The Lens Collective

A Guide to Seeing Different Perspectives in Project Management

Association for Project Management

Association for Project Management
Ibis House, Regent Park
Summerleys Road
Princes Risborough
Buckinghamshire
HP27 9LE

© Association for Project Management 2010

No part of this publication may be reproduced, stored in a retrieval system or transmitted in any form, or by any means without the permission in writing from the Association for Project Management. Within the United Kingdom, exceptions are allowed in respect of fair dealing for the purposes of research or private study, or criticism or review as permitted under the Copyright, Designs and Patents Act, 1988 providing that the source is acknowledged clearly and near to the cited text, including the name of the association, the title of the publication and the place and date of the publication. Enquiries concerning reproduction outside these terms and in other countries should be sent to the publishing department of the Association for Project Management at the address above.

Readers are responsible for the correct application of the information in this publication and its conformity with all relevant legal and commercial obligations. The Association for Project Management cannot accept legal responsibility or liability for any errors or omissions in this publication or the consequences thereof.

British Library Cataloguing in Publication Data is available

ISBN 10: 1-903494-31-1
ISBN 13: 978-1-903494-31-8

Cover design by Fountainhead Creative Consultants

Typeset by RefineCatch Limited, Bungay, Suffolk

Contents

Acknowledgements	iv
Foreword	v
The lens collective	1
Lenses	
Benefiting from people in projects	4
Applying governance in projects	6
Project stakeholders	8
Multi-cultural project management	10
Project planning	12
Risk management in projects	14
Project communication	16
Negotiating within projects	18
Project contracts and procurement	20
Harnessing conflict in projects	22
Leveraging creativity in projects	24
Bibliography	**26**

Acknowledgements

In creating *The Lens Collective*, the APM People Significant Interest Group (SIG) invited input from other SIGs. The APM People SIG conducted workshops with SIG representatives to reflect upon the people aspects within their respective disciplines.

The Association for Project Management would like to acknowledge and extend appreciation for all the contributions from:

- The editorial team
  - Irene MacDonald
  - Rob Sadler
  - Sheilina Somani

- The working group
  - Donnie MacNicol
  - David Hart
  - Bob Newman
  - Troy Buckley

- The APM People SIG Members

- Representatives from the following APM Specific Interest Groups
  - The APM Risk SIG
  - The APM Planning SIG
  - The APM Contracts and Procurement SIG
  - The APM Governance SIG

- Transport for London (TfL), London Rail for their generous hospitality.

Foreword

We believe that individuals will use the lens collective to reflect upon their capabilities, increase their awareness of others and successfully apply new perspectives to their projects.

IRENE MACDONALD FAPM

As a project management professional, Irene is an APM member and has been a Fellow since 2007. She is a book reviewer for *Project* magazine, a committee member for the APM People SIG and the APM SIG Steering Group, a judge for the APM Awards, a guest lecturer at Kingston University and a public speaker on people and culture in change and project management. "I have long held the view that people, rather than processes, make the difference in project success."

ROB SADLER

As a seasoned project management executive, Rob has been an APM member since 1997 and has attained the APM Practitioner Qualification. He is a committee member of the APM People SIG and, through his work at TfL, hosts their meetings and workshops. "I became involved in the APM People SIG and subsequently this working group because I feel passionately that people and their various facets are prime enablers in the success of project management."

SHEILINA SOMANI FAPM

As an international project management speaker on 'tough skills' and diversity integration, she has always promoted the notion that project management *is* people management. She is both an APM member and Fellow. She is a book reviewer for *Project* magazine, a regular article contributor, a committee member for the APM People SIG and member of the examining review panel. "I joined this experienced team intending to add to the richness of dimensions and perceptions we seek to share."

We undertook the production of this lens booklet with passion and trepidation. We started by considering the strategy we needed in order to achieve success. We settled on a simple start, stop, continue approach; keeping to three key principals in each area. Below is an outline strategy we used, which we believe contributed to this successful outcome.

START
- Clear, defined outcomes and intended audience.
- A project plan, change log and individual commitment.
- Strong, determined and passionate individuals.

STOP
- Avoid procrastination.
- Limit team size to maximise effectiveness.
- Don't reinvent the wheel each time we meet.

CONTINUE
- Commit to a schedule and adhere to it.
- Channel creativity, humour and discourse.
- Express thoughts, opinions and values openly and honestly.

During this project we pooled our energy and knowledge, engaged in lively discussions and developed solutions. We conclude this project with great satisfaction and a tinge of regret that the work is complete. However, we look forward to the opportunity to work together as a team again soon.

The lens collective

PERSPECTIVE

The term 'lens' has been specifically chosen for this guide to reflect the analogy between human vision and the interaction of people. This context also facilitates the analogy between the tools and techniques used to enhance, correct, protect and improve this interaction.

The eye is the vehicle through which the brain understands distance, shape, form, colour, shade, light, dark, and dimensions. These are based upon frames of reference shaped by, for example:

- culture and beliefs;
- values and ethics;
- experience and upbringing;
- preferences and prejudices;
- education and influences;
- context and external factors;
- perceived opportunity and risk;
- mood and behaviours.

Throughout our lifetime, our vision evolves, becoming stronger or weaker. Sometimes intervention is required in the form of glasses, contact lenses or surgery. Equally, our own frames of reference evolve over time, adapting and reshaping through exposure to variety.

The human dimension gives each of us the capacity to choose to evolve according to our circumstances. We have the ability to employ tools to refine our perspectives. We can identify which corrective action may prove useful and implement effective tools. When seeking to improve or correct vision, we determine the type and intensity of lens required in conjunction with the existing range of products, such as glasses, telescope, microscope, periscope, magnifying glass, endoscope, night-sight or sunglasses.

In project, programme and portfolio management, there are infinite and complex human dimensions. This guide offers lenses to enhance, correct, protect and improve relationships, behaviours and outcomes within these environments.

GUIDELINES

The APM People SIG was formed to acknowledge that the most complex aspect of project management is people. We seek to emphasise the people dimensions of many recognised areas within project management, i.e. procurement, risk, governance, planning, etc. Specific processes, tools and techniques within these areas may be garnered from the appropriate APM SIGs.

The Lens Collective

Defining the lens collective

- It is a suite of tools providing thought provoking questions centred upon people.
- It represents knowledge capture of project management from practitioners, subject matter experts and academics.
- It encourages project managers to reflect and consider alternative courses of behaviour.
- It enables project managers to utilise those aspects that are pertinent to their current circumstances.
- It provides a context, summary question and series of challenges to assess the current status.
- It prompts individuals to expand their understanding and analysis of project challenges or contexts.
- It creates opportunity to widen knowledge to diagnose and respond to particular conditions.
- Each 'lens' employed can also be utilised to close out issues, phases and the project itself.
- It presents insights to pertinent issues that may be alleviated through employing it.

The lens collective is intended for:

- inexperienced, upcoming, learning or junior project managers;
- project managers who are experiencing people related difficulties;
- project managers who are primarily process orientated;
- experienced project, programme and portfolio managers who want to increase their perspectives;
- mentors, trainers, coaches and programme managers to use as a facilitation tool.

The purpose of providing the lens collective is to facilitate:

- a focus upon people;
- the evolution of perspectives;
- access to alternative frames of reference for greater understanding;
- the need to balance people with process;
- promotion of communication to incorporate different approaches;
- success through people using flexible enablers;
- expansion of personal competence.

Benefits of applying the lens collective:

- It helps to probe the latent power of people.
- It enables higher levels of self-awareness.
- It encourages project managers to increase their individual effectiveness.
- It empowers project managers to greater flexibility in people management.
- It leverages collective experience and knowledge.
- It provokes dialogue.
- It facilitates the identification of root causes of problems.

- It promotes creative problem solving.
- It provides insights that may assist in addressing issues.
- It enables collaborative teamwork.

The lens collective is proffered in the context of challenging established paradigms or terms of reference:

- The content is intended to be thought provoking or reflective.
- The language is intentionally accessible and everyday.
- The rhetorical style of questions aims to promote independent thought and action.
- The lenses can be used wholly, sequentially, partially or uniquely.
- In a specific lens, it may be that a single question proves relevant or appropriate.
- Each question can be utilised at any point throughout the project or programme lifecycle.

Health warnings

- The lens collective is not a panacea.
- The lens collective is not a checklist or definitive process.
- The lens collective is not exhaustive.
- The lens collective is not academic, nor does it claim to have new or emerging theories.

Pre-requisites for applying the lens collective

- Open minded approach – flexibility and awareness that options exist.
- Preparation – requires time and effort.
- Personal cognisance – attitude, preferences and motivation.
- Framing – recognise uniqueness of each situation or context.
- Judicial thought – the ability to discern current state, motivation, potential to apply lens.
- Outcome orientation – what you hope to achieve.

Using the lens collective

- The lens collective is universally applicable, regardless of the complexity of the project, programme or portfolio.
- The lens collective can be deployed from the outset of the project.
- The lens collective can be used iteratively through the project or programme lifecycle.
- Individual 'lenses' can be applied during the project or programme lifecycle.
- Each 'lens' can be utilised wholly or partially.
- Each 'lens' can be applied individually or collaboratively.
- Each 'lens' can be used for self or group reflection.
- Each 'lens' can be applied to inspire, motivate and enhance people performance.

The Lens Collective

| **Lens 01 :**

 Benefiting from people in projects | **Summary question:**

 "What questions do I need to ask in order to understand and achieve success through the people contributing to the project?" |

This lens is about understanding the value people bring to the project.

This lens can help you to:

- take time on your own to reflect on your perceived skill set;
- incorporate a variety of people when forming, developing and evolving a project team;
- facilitate openness through discussion of the lens content with colleagues;
- increase your awareness of the varied dimensions of people;
- reduce the potential for hidden agendas;
- evolve respect for the impact people have in the project context.

Areas this can help you address:

- Increasing motivation and commitment to the project.
- Understanding and managing the varied perceptions and expectations of team members.
- Assessing the impact of conflicting priorities and requirements of team members.
- Creating confidence of people in working as a project team.
- Influencing the culture of your organisation to create a better environment for success.
- Increasing stakeholder confidence and trust in meeting their expectations.

Questions to ask:

1. Do I understand the critical elements of working with people?

- Am I able to define the range of motivational factors?
- Do I understand that individuals vary in what motivates them?
- Do I appreciate that individuals have an inherent hierarchy of need?
- What are the dominant cultural influences; individual, geographic, organisational?
- Do I understand how the objectives/outcomes of the project relate to each individual?
- Do I understand the varied communication styles and preferences of the members of the project team?

- Do I understand the range of styles/preferences of working environments?
- Do I understand the individual learning styles and development cycles?
- Do I understand how all of the above points influence team dynamics?

2. **How can I maximise the value people bring to the project?**
   - Am I able to define my own preferences?
   - Am I able to approach the subject without imposing pre-judged outcomes?
   - Am I able to empathise?
   - How well do I lead by example through appropriate behaviour?
   - Am I able to relate to the range of preferences of others?
   - Am I flexible in my approach to communication, processes and outcomes?
   - Am I able to blend the range of styles to create a team?
   - How well do I recognise limitations in individual performance and/or attitude?
   - Am I able to apply leadership and management skills effectively?

3. **How do I ensure that I optimise the value of people I interact with?**
   - Can I respond to the varying needs for recognition and reward?
   - How well can I inspire and sustain an environment of openness, honesty and trust?
   - Am I confident to apply a range of leadership styles?
   - Am I responsive to individual needs for affiliation?
   - How well can I demonstrate confidence in individuals through flexible leadership?
   - Am I able to effectively tailor deployment of individuals to the needs of the project?

4. **What can be done to overcome challenges?**
   - Am I sufficiently detached to be objective about the challenge presented?
   - Am I able to identify the principal source of the challenge?
   - Who else can be brought in to help, diffuse or evolve the challenge?
   - Is the challenge critical enough to warrant a change of personnel?

The Lens Collective

Lens 02: **Applying governance in projects**	**Summary question:** *"What questions do I need to ask in order to understand and achieve success through establishing and maintaining integrated governance to fulfil both organisational and project requirements?"*

This lens is about effective governance in the project context.

This lens can help you to:

- empower your team through structure and guidance;
- understand the fit with other projects, programmes and corporate strategy;
- assist with clarity in stakeholder responsibilities;
- help you appreciate the extent of your influence within the governance context.

Areas this can help you address:

- Using the governance model where conflict, misinformation or issues arise.
- Building confidence and consistency within the project.
- Engagement and visibility of key stakeholders.
- Understanding how your project fits within the existing programme or portfolio.
- Influencing project governance.
- Management of expectations.

Questions to ask:

1. Do I understand the critical elements of governance?

- Do I understand the business portfolio?
- Do I understand the regulatory and compliance requirements?
- Am I aware of any specific sensitivity or confidentiality aspects?
- Am I aware of external factors that may influence the direction of corporate strategy?
- What do the team believe are the benefits of the governance strategy?
- Do external parties use the same governance processes?
- How can I ensure that there is consistency of governance between all parties?
- Do I understand how governance influences completion and success criteria?
- Are the parameters for realisation of business benefits clearly defined?
- How does my project fit into the corporate strategy?
- Have I identified who has ultimate power and authority over deliverables and outcomes?
- Have the authorisation points and audit criteria been clearly defined?

2. **Do I have the requisite knowledge and experience to apply corporate governance?**
    - Do I appreciate the distinction between my organisation's governance of project management and governance of this project?
    - Do I understand how this project originated?
    - Do I understand my responsibilities in establishing good governance?
    - Do I understand the roles and responsibilities of the sponsor and their deputy?
    - Do I know the established escalation routes?
    - Can I articulate the established governance processes to all stakeholders?
    - Does the project management methodology support governance?
    - Am I confident to challenge authority and in turn be challenged?

3. **How do I implement supportive governance practices?**
    - Have I reached agreement with the sponsor on their level of engagement and visibility?
    - Do I have the skills and confidence to manage the wider stakeholder group?
    - How do I facilitate team confidence in the governance framework?
    - Do I need a checklist to ensure I address appropriate governance requirements?
    - How do I ensure that the business case retains relevance throughout the project?
    - Am I able to align perceived conflicts in articulated objectives?
    - How am I going to generate and sustain open relationships across all stakeholders?
    - What do I need to do to maintain confidence of senior stakeholders?

4. **What can be done to ensure that the governance process is enabling?**
    - How can I apply boundaries to ensure that governance does not become restrictive?
    - Are the critical parameters identified and regularly reported upon?
    - How do I foster a no-blame environment to encourage openness?
    - How do I validate reported information for quality and consistency?
    - How do I facilitate open and frank disclosure throughout the governance structure?

The Lens Collective

Lens 03:	Summary question:
Project stakeholders	*"What questions do I need to ask in order to understand and achieve success as seen from the perspectives of key project stakeholders?"*

This lens is about understanding key stakeholder perspectives and their impact on the project.

This lens can help you to:

- understand and manage stakeholder perspectives in the project context;
- include stakeholder perspectives in planning, delivering and concluding projects;
- incorporate these activities when planning, estimating and costing a project;
- influence the effect of politics in projects.

Areas this can help you address:

- Management of variable, and often hidden, personal agendas of stakeholders.
- Conflict between stakeholders regarding perceptions and expectations.
- Stakeholder confidence and trust in the project.
- Improving the competence and confidence of the project team in stakeholder management.

Questions to ask:

1. Do I understand the critical elements of stakeholder management?

- What are the politics surrounding this project?
- Am I able to identify the stakeholders and their stance in relation to the project?
- Which stakeholders have the greatest influence on project success or failure?
- Do I understand the multiple agendas that may be present?
- What are the prevailing implicit and explicit expectations?
- Who owns the final project outcomes?
- Are the resource providers and end users recognised and included as stakeholders?
- Is there a stakeholder map?
- Are the individual project team members recognised on the stakeholder map?
- How likely is it that key stakeholders will change during the life of the project?
- Are there alternate stakeholders from whom I can actively solicit support?
- Is there time and money allocated specifically to manage stakeholders effectively?

2. How can I proactively manage stakeholders during the project?

- Am I confident to orchestrate stakeholder interactions?
- Am I able to proactively manage stakeholder expectations?
- Do I appreciate the range of perspectives, values and beliefs influencing stakeholder behaviour?
- Can I elicit assumptions that are driving stakeholder behaviours?
- Do I understand stakeholder perspectives will evolve/change over time?
- Can I align objectives, outcomes and success criteria amongst stakeholders?
- Am I confident to manage stakeholder conflict scenarios?

3. How do I maximise the value of stakeholder management?

- Have I planned to actively manage stakeholders and their perspectives?
- Do I have appropriate mechanisms to sustain stakeholder engagement?
- How will I effectively monitor fluctuations in importance, priority of stakeholders?
- How will I ensure that completion criteria and expectations are regularly reassessed?
- How well am I able to draw out implicit expectations to determine their appropriateness?

4. What can be done if stakeholder engagement breaks down?

- Do I have defined routes for negotiation, escalation and potentially to stop the project?
- Have the organisational objectives moved or changed significantly?
- Do I need to re-energise the stakeholder community?
- Do need to revise my strategies, mechanisms for stakeholder management?
- Do I need to assess whether the project is still viable to the stakeholders?

Lens 04:	Summary question:
Multi-cultural project management	*"What questions do I need to ask in order to understand and achieve success through effective cultural awareness within my project?"*

This lens is about cultural relationship management in the project context.

This lens can help you to:

- facilitate cultural awareness in teams;
- identify key strengths and weaknesses relating to managing culture;
- consciously manage cultural dimensions, both individually and in teams;
- consider the needs of other parties and to act accordingly in a professional way.

Areas this can help you address:

- Improving your understanding of culture, diversity and similarities.
- Gaining higher levels of confidence when managing teams.
- Improving your observation and listening skills and applied learning.
- Strengthening your team dynamics through leveraging culture.
- Increasing your ability to successfully manage global teams.
- Increasing cultural awareness of team members for their future effectiveness.

Questions to ask:

1. Do I understand the critical elements of culture?

- Do I understand the dimensions of culture: values, beliefs, behaviours, symbols?
- Do I have sufficient insight of the range of cultures within the team?
- Am I aware of assumptions and prejudices that drive individual behaviour?
- Do I understand the importance of setting a project climate for behaviour?
- Do I understand how to leverage cultural awareness to develop teamwork?
- Am I able to promote cultural similarities whilst respecting diversity?
- Do I have any critical sensitivities that need to be actively managed?
- Am I able to articulate that cultural diversity relates to communication/interaction?
- Does my planning take into account a good work-life balance, external commitments of team members?

2. **How can I be an effective project manager from a cultural perspective?**
    - Am I competent to engage the team in open exploration of their cultures?
    - Am I able to suspend my personal prejudices and assumptions?
    - Do I have the ability to create a team culture based on behaviours, language and interaction?
    - Am I able to manage both my own emotions and those of others?
    - Do I have sufficient knowledge or information to engage multiple cultures successfully?
    - Am I able to use a variety of communication tools?
    - Do I have the skills to effectively elicit what is important for individuals and for the team?
    - Am I able to role model culturally appropriate behaviours?
    - Does the working hours expectation adequately respect individual needs?

3. **How do I consistently support cultural dimensions within my project?**
    - Am I able to make most effective use of individual and team preferences?
    - Am I confident enough to confront cultural issues and resolve them?
    - Am I ensuring that religious practices, festivals and holidays are being respected?
    - Do I consistently support appropriate behaviours?
    - Am I confident to react to and correct inappropriate behaviour?
    - Do I need to present information in more concise language?
    - Have I included culture as a topic in project learning and review sessions?
    - Am I able to provide a forum to enable team members to manage their prejudices?

4. **What can be done when agreement cannot be reached?**
    - Am I able to actively manage cultural conflict?
    - Do I know who to gain advice from when cultural conflict arises?
    - Do I understand the legal processes that need to be observed?
    - Am I able to draw on professional resources to escalate and resolve cultural issues?

The Lens Collective

Lens 05:	Summary question:
Project planning	*"What questions do I need to ask in order to understand and achieve success through effective project planning?"*

This lens is about effective planning in the project context.

This lens can help you to:

- understand the factors that influence effective planning;
- appreciate that planning is a continuous and evolving process;
- inculcate the dimensions of people, documentation and processes into effective planning.

Areas this can help you address:

- Raising awareness of considerations for planning.
- Increasing planning effectiveness.
- Raising visibility of risks.
- Recognising opportunities.
- Managing stakeholder expectations.
- Increasing the quality of your planning.

Questions to ask:

1. **Do I understand the critical elements of planning?**
    - Do I understand the purpose of planning?
    - Do I understand the totality of the planning process, the strategic nature of planning, stakeholder management and the production of documentation?
    - Are there existing procedures or funding/approval cycles that will influence planning?
    - What has been approved/funded (e.g. feasibility study, planning phase or project)?
    - Are stakeholder expectations congruent with the initial planning process?
    - Do I understand the project constraints, objectives and completion criteria?
    - Are there external factors to consider?
    - How will the project plan be communicated to the stakeholders?
    - Is the planning approach suitable for this project?
    - How well do the elements of the project plan reflect reporting requirements?
    - Do I understand how progress and achievement will be measured?
    - Do I understand that planning complexity, detail and approaches will vary during the project life cycle?

2. **How can I influence the project through effective planning?**
   - Do I have the requisite skills and experiences required to effectively plan this project?
   - Am I able to apply appropriate tools and techniques to capture, communicate and report planning vs actual achievement?
   - How well do I involve the team in the setting of the milestones?
   - Have I identified the major milestones that anchor the project?
   - Have I planned and committed time for active and continuous project planning?
   - Can I apply appropriate planning techniques to reflect requirements and project phases?
   - How well do I use the planning process to communicate the project tasks?
   - Have I included planning for individual commitments (e.g. holidays, personal events, etc.)?

3. **How do I leverage project planning for team effectiveness?**
   - Am I able to ensure that the members of my team understand the positive role of project planning?
   - Am I able to create an environment conducive to the sharing of information, knowledge, concerns and dependencies?
   - Can I employ an appropriate range of tools/techniques to facilitate effective planning?
   - Am I enforcing the need to actively manage project planning and replanning?
   - Does the plan reflect the changing nature of the project?
   - Are stakeholder expectations actively managed to align with project planning?
   - Am I communicating the accuracy of the project plan with respect to milestones, critical path and project outcomes?
   - Does our planning accurately reflect financial drivers for spending and allocations?
   - Does our planning adequately incorporate project risk?

4. **What can be done if the project planning process falters?**
   - Am I able to revisit my planning processes to test their suitability for the project phase?
   - Is the project plan detail aligned with the current phase (e.g. detail/high level)?
   - Am I able to establish whether the challenge is due to internal people issues and/or process?
   - Are there external factors impinging on the project environment?
   - Am I able to create a 'time out' space to reconsider the appropriateness of the plan?
   - Is there a need to reposition stakeholder expectations?
   - Is it necessary to 'pause' the project to replan?
   - Is escalation necessary to pause the project, manage constraints and resolve planning issues?

The Lens Collective

Lens 06:	Summary question:
Risk management in projects	*"What questions do I need to ask in order to understand and achieve success through leveraging risk management in the project context?"*

This lens is about understanding risk management and its impact on the project.

This lens can help you to:

- understand the value of risk management in the project context;
- understand the pivotal importance of your role in risk management;
- encourage people to include threat and opportunity management throughout the project;
- incorporate risk management activities when planning, estimating and costing a project.

Areas this can help you address:

- Increasing stakeholder confidence and trust in risk management.
- Improving the competence of the project team through risk management.
- Managing fluctuating risk events, both positive and negative, and their outcomes.
- Providing a forum for honest and open dialogue of expectations and experience.
- Reducing surprises.

Questions to ask:

1. Do I understand the critical elements of risk management?

- Do I understand the value of risk management?
- What is the current organisational risk management strategy?
- Am I able to differentiate between risks within my control versus those that are not?
- Are stakeholders committed to ownership of, and responsibility for, risk management?
- Do I recognise that threat and opportunity both belong in risk management?
- Do I understand how the project risk profile evolves and/or changes over time?
- Do I appreciate that risks are influenced by perspective, preferences and experience?
- Have I planned and committed time for continuous risk management?
- Do I have clearly defined boundaries for my authority in managing risk?

2. **How can I proactively manage risk during the project?**
    - Am I able to create a climate of open/honest contribution to facilitate risk management?
    - Am I able to ensure my team understand the positive role of risk management?
    - Am I aware of the value of reviewing lessons learned and leveraging experience?
    - Am I able to ensure I do not impose my personal perspective of risks?
    - How well do I communicate my feelings in relation to risk?
    - Am I consciously including individual stakeholder risks (e.g. family or religious events)?
    - Am I able to apply corporate risk strategies to this project?
    - Am I able to effectively communicate the differences between risks and issues?
    - Can I employ an appropriate range of tools/techniques to facilitate risk management?
    - Am I confident to present risk management directly/honestly at senior levels?

3. **How do I maximise the value of risk management?**
    - Am I visibly demonstrating leadership and ownership of risk management?
    - How open-minded am I to alternative approaches, expressions and solutions?
    - Are there nominated individuals to deputise in case of absence?
    - Am I enforcing the need to regularly and actively manage risk?
    - Am I facilitating recognition of responsibility for risk amongst the team?
    - Am I accessible enough for team members to approach with emerging risks?
    - Am I consistent in supporting contribution rather than apportioning blame?
    - Am I able to actively manage polarised opinions on risk (extreme aversion/immersion)?
    - Have I prepared stakeholders for the outcomes of honest/truthful contribution?
    - Am I leveraging timely involvement from key stakeholders?

4. **What can be done when major risks materialise?**
    - Am I confident to implement my authority in executing response strategies?
    - Am I able to authorise pursuit/exploitation of opportunity?
    - Am I confident in seeking help in risk management?
    - Am I able to apply criteria to pause/stop the project whilst risks are addressed?
    - Do I have accessible routes to escalate issues for resolution?
    - Do I have defined exit strategies that can be readily deployed?

The Lens Collective

| Lens 07:

Project communication | **Summary question:**

"What questions do I need to ask in order to understand and achieve success through effective communications within my project?" |

This lens is about effective project communication.

This lens can help you to:

- affirm your ability to communicate effectively;
- build relationships with key stakeholders;
- communicate clarity of project objectives and targets across the team;
- minimise misunderstandings;
- influence the interests of key stakeholders;
- increase stakeholder confidence and trust.

Areas this can help you address:

- Understanding of politics within the project environment.
- Key stakeholders who may have a "hidden agenda".
- Understanding of cultural issues, including the values and beliefs that an organisation holds.
- Language coherence: clarity of speech, use of acronyms and vocabulary, pace and attitude.
- Diversity of learning styles: verbal, auditory, visual, kinaesthetic.
- Creating collaborative project teams.

Questions to ask:

1. **Do I understand the critical elements of communication?**
    - Am I able to articulate the purpose and relevance of communication?
    - Do I understand the diversity of cultures and learning styles of the stakeholders?
    - Do I understand the range of communication styles?
    - Do I understand the relative effectiveness of communication methods?
    - Do I understand the difference between urgency and timeliness?
    - Am I cognisant of the communication model for transmission/receipt/understanding?
    - Do I understand the different forums required for formal, informal, public and confidential interactions?

2. How can I be an effective role model for communication?
- Can I actively listen?
- Am I able to focus on the communication and exclude distractions?
- Can I empathise appropriately?
- Am I aware of how to use body language?
- Am I flexible in my approach to communications among stakeholders?
- Am I able to adapt to other stakeholder communication preferences?
- Do I need a communication plan?

3. How do I facilitate effective communication?
- Have I conducted a stakeholder analysis and identified all the key stakeholders?
- Have I established the purpose of the proposed communications?
- Is the information relevant to the stakeholders I am communicating with?
- Do I have a communication plan in place with a timeline for meetings, etc?
- Am I able to communicate across different styles and media?
- Am I able to employ diverse delivery styles within the team?
- Am I managing diversity of time zones, locations, cultures and media preferences?
- Am I testing for understanding, commitment and agreement to what I'm proposing?

4. What can be done to address the complexities of communication?
- What are the limitations of the types of media and can you overcome them?
- Am I aware of the cost and time relationships of different communication approaches?
- Am I able to read body language effectively to address potential miscommunication?
- Do I have sufficient acuity to accurately interpret what is being communicated to me?
- Am I able to communicate sufficient information without overwhelming volume?
- Am I disciplined enough to capture the content of diverse communication?

The Lens Collective

Lens 08:	Summary question:
Negotiating within projects	*"What questions do I need to ask in order to understand and achieve success through effective negotiation within my project?"*

This lens is about effective negotiation in the project context.

This lens can help you to:

- prepare yourself better for negotiations within your projects;
- identify your key strengths and weaknesses relating to effective negotiations;
- think about negotiations as a means to resolving conflicts successfully;
- consider the needs of other parties and to act accordingly in a professional way.

Areas this can help you address:

- Improving any negotiation skills gap you may have identified.
- Gaining higher levels of confidence when negotiating with other parties.
- Improving your observation and listening skills.
- Improving your planning and people skills.

Questions to ask:

1. **Do I understand the critical elements of negotiation?**
   - Do I understand the context of the negotiation?
   - Do I have sufficient insight to the agenda – both overt and hidden?
   - Am I aware of the constraints of time, money and outcomes?
   - Do I understand the objectives, motives and needs of all parties?
   - Do I understand what each party would consider a win?
   - What do I need to do to enable each party to achieve a win?
   - Is this the appropriate time to address this negotiation?
   - Are the appropriate people available to conduct this negotiation?

2. **How can I be an effective negotiator?**
   - Am I able to suspend my personal preferences to facilitate the negotiation?
   - Am I able to manage both my own emotions and those of others?
   - Do I have sufficient knowledge or information to negotiate successfully?
   - Do I understand the need for adequate preparation prior to negotiations?
   - How confident am I to lead the negotiations?
   - Have I considered the needs of the parties I need to negotiate with?

- Do I understand the elements, techniques and strategies of successful negotiations?
- Am I confident to summon additional resources if required?
- How well do I communicate with others in negotiations?

3. **How do I conduct negotiations?**
    - Am I able to make most effective use of time, breaks and space?
    - Am I confident with confrontation?
    - Do I know how willing the other party is to collaborate?
    - Do I know how I can evolve conflict to seek agreement?
    - Do I understand how to establish concessions to achieve a compromise?
    - Do I know when and how to apply exit strategies; deferred authority, arbitration and escalation?

4. **What can be done when agreement cannot be reached?**
    - Am I prepared for the negotiation to fail?
    - Do I understand how to facilitate a 'walk away'?
    - Do I have a process for communicating the outcome of the negotiation?
    - Do I understand how to leverage the dialogue from the negotiation?

The Lens Collective

Lens 09:	**Summary question:**
Project contracts and procurement	*"What questions do I need to ask in order to understand and achieve success through effective contract/procurement management in my project?"*

This lens is about effectively directing contracts and procurement in the project context.

This lens can help you to:

- reinforce the importance of consistent behaviour through applied contract management;
- improve your understanding of relationship management as a contract enabler;
- recognise the contract as an enabler and working tool for project success;
- confirm the importance of tracking interim milestones and final deliverables;
- confirm that contract expediting is a driving force for project completion.

Areas this can help you address:

- Increasing your understanding of contract management.
- Applying wider stakeholder management to achieve contract success.
- Strengthening your project delivery through change control and contract management.

Questions to ask:

1. Do I understand the critical elements of project contracts/procurement?

- Do I understand the contracts/procurement process for my project?
- Do I understand that the contract forms the foundation, framework and fallback for all parties?
- Do I have sufficient knowledge of contract law or access to appropriate advice?
- Is my contract primarily for service or deliverables?
- Does the contract adequately define the completion criteria?
- Do I understand the balance of procured vs internally resourced individuals?
- Have we defined adequate soft/hard milestones for continuous contract management?
- Do I understand the contractual dependency (tender/preferred or sole supplier status)?
- Am I able to clearly identify the requirements, desires and dreams of the stakeholders?
- Is there an established contractual relationship and history?

- Do I understand the PM role and responsibilities for this contract?
- Is the change control process clearly defined?
- Is there capacity within the contract/procurement process for negotiation?
- Do I understand the project constraints defined within the contract?
- Do I understand the means for contract re-negotiation?

2. **How can I leverage contract/procurement for successful project outcomes?**
   - Do I have access to procurement and legal representatives to maintain and deliver to this contract?
   - Do I have a strong working relationship with representatives of other parties?
   - Can I establish what the critical aspects to the contractual orientation?
   - Do I understand the critical path?
   - Am I able to create an environment to enable external parties to co-own the project?
   - Am I able to influence the management of external parties?
   - Am I able to articulate the level of collaboration required by all parties?
   - Am I able to effectively challenge milestone achievements?
   - Can I influence the selection of external resources critical to my project?
   - Am I able to clearly allocate appropriate risk ownership across multiple parties?

3. **How do I proactively leverage the contract/procurement process?**
   - Am I able to role model contractual focus and consistent behaviour in all situations?
   - How do I develop and sustain professional relationships with all parties?
   - Have I organised a multi-party team meeting to kick of the project?
   - Have we established common objectives across all contributing parties?
   - Am I able to remain outcome-focused, and therefore open to alternative solutions?
   - Is there a change control process established and communicated to all parties?
   - Do I have a comprehensive project plan illustrating all the inter-dependencies?
   - Has the critical path been clearly illustrated and articulated to all parties?
   - Do I have a tracking mechanism for interim deliverables?
   - Do I have an established process for actively expediting contract deliverables?
   - Am I actively managing contractual risks?

4. **What can be done when contractual relationships falter/fail?**
   - Am I able to invoke a spirit of partnership to seek resolution prior to escalation?
   - Do I understand the route for conflict resolution, escalation and potential arbitration?
   - Are there clear penalty and/or break clauses that need to be invoked?
   - Do I have access to appropriate legal counsel if required?

The Lens Collective

Lens 10: **Harnessing conflict in projects**	**Summary question:** *"What questions do I need to ask in order to understand and achieve success through harnessing conflict in my project?"*

This lens is about effectively leveraging conflict in the project context.

This lens can help you to:

- view conflict positively;
- accept that there will be conflicts which require intervention;
- focus on root causes of conflict as opposed to treatment of symptoms;
- position conflict proactively within the project environment;
- acknowledge that conflict in projects exists and can be actively addressed;
- facilitate a 'no blame' culture, encouraging openness and honesty.

Areas this can help you address:

- Increased confidence in managing conflict.
- Strengthening team dynamics.
- Improve individual behaviour and identify learning and development needs.
- Application of strong leadership skills.

Questions to ask:

1. Do I understand the critical elements of conflict?

- Do I appreciate the difference between disagreement and conflict?
- Do I understand the potential causes of conflict?
- Do I understand how to identify early warning signs?
- Can I identify who the conflicted parties are?
- Is there a history of conflict between the parties?
- How will conflict affect the project life cycle and outcomes?
- Do I understand that conflict has both personal and professional dimensions?
- Am I able to discern any political influences?
- Do I understand that emotion plays a significant role in conflict?
- Do I understand facets of resolution, including arbitration, escalation and negotiation?

2. How can I harness conflict in projects?

- Am I confident when faced with conflict?
- Am I able to modify my behaviour to effectively manage conflict?
- Am I able to differentiate between overt and hidden agendas?
- Can I employ appropriate logic, emotion and pragmatism in conflict scenarios?
- Can I facilitate acceptance, collaboration or willingness to accommodate?
- Can I take a confrontational approach when necessary?

3. How do I proactively harness conflict?

- How can I encourage use of reflection to facilitate understanding?
- How can I time intervention to the best effect?
- Am I able to effectively apply appropriate negotiation strategies?
- Am I able to exploit dimensions of physical space?
- Am I able to leverage patterns of behaviour?
- Am I able to employ approaches ranging from provocation to acquiescence?

4. What can be done when conflict cannot be resolved?

- Am I able to trade contributing elements to alleviate conflict?
- Is it possible to adjourn from the conflict?
- Am I able to garner support from others?
- Can the conflict be readily escalated?
- Is it possible to contain the conflict without the project being impacted?

The Lens Collective

Lens 11:	**Summary question:**
Leveraging creativity in projects	*"What questions do I need to ask in order to understand and achieve success through leveraging creativity and innovation in my projects?"*

This lens is about encouraging and harnessing creativity and innovation in projects.

This lens can help you to:

- create new ideas of how to improve project performance and delivery;
- manage and deliver projects more creatively;
- inspire and stimulate stakeholders;
- motivate individuals for professional and personal development;
- help facilitate competitive advantage.

Areas this can help you address:

- Applying innovation where traditional methods are no longer achieving the required outcomes.
- Issues affecting project delivery.
- Enhancing established practices and behaviours.
- Stifled creativity and innovation in the organisation.
- Absence of confidence to implement new ways of working.

Questions to ask:

1. **Do I understand the critical elements of creativity and innovation?**
   - Am I able to define 'out-of-the-box' thinking?
   - Can I define creative problem solving and innovative approaches to others?
   - Do I understand how to look at things from a different perspective?
   - Have I considered my organisation's capacity for creativity and innovation?
   - Have I considered the range of creativity and innovation within the team?
   - How can I support corporate strategy by being innovative in project delivery?

2. **How can I encourage and harness creativity in my project?**
   - Do I feel comfortable with creativity and innovation?
   - Do I understand what can be done differently in my project?
   - Am I employing creativity and innovation appropriately?
   - Do I understand how to stimulate creativity and innovation?
   - Do I feel confident in facilitating constructive conflict to achieve creativity?

- Do I have the necessary tools and techniques to apply innovation?
- Do I understand how to manage the creativity of others?
- Can I create and sustain confidence with stakeholders?

3. **How do I identify scope for creativity and innovation in my project?**
    - Can I define the opportunities for innovation?
    - Can I articulate the boundaries for applying innovation?
    - Have I identified strategies to sustain and manage creativity?
    - How will I effectively manage risks and issues arising from creative approaches?
    - Do I have access to additional resources to support creativity and innovation?
    - How can I modify key performance indicators to accommodate innovation?
    - How do I convert creativity and innovation into project delivery and closeout?

4. **What can be done to respond to extremes in creativity and innovation?**
    - Am I able to articulate and apply lessons learned to increase responsiveness?
    - Can I channel or redirect creativity to sustain project direction?
    - Am I able to curtail excessive creativity?
    - Do I know which parties to escalate to?
    - Am I confident in pausing progress to reinforce innovation boundaries?

Bibliography

Buckingham, M. and Coffman, *First, Break All the Rules*, Simon & Schuster (2005)

De Board, Robert., *The Psychoanalysis of Organisations.* Routledge (1978)

Gallwey, T., *The Inner Game of Tennis*, Random House (1974)

Gladwell, Malcolm., *The Tipping Point*. Little, Brown and Company (2002)

Gladwell, Malcolm., *The Outliers*. Little, Brown and Company (2008)

Jandt, Fred. E., *An Introduction to Intercultural Communication* 4ed. Sage Publications (2004)

Molden, D., *Managing with the power of NLP*, 2nd Edition, Pearson Education (1996)

O' Connor, J. and Lages, A., *How coaching works*, A&C Black (2004)

Pellerin, Charles., *How NASA Builds Teams*, John Wiley and Sons, (2009)

Tufte, E.R., *The Visual Display of Quantitative Information*, 2nd Edition, Graphics Press (2001)